Mechanic Mike's M...

Diggers

Franklin Watts
This edition published in the UK in 2016 by The Watts Publishing Group

Copyright © 2014 David West Children's Books

Designed and illustrated by David West

Dewey number 629.2'25
PB ISBN: 978 1 4451 5178 6

Printed in Malaysia

Franklin Watts
An imprint of
Hachette Children's Group
Part of The Watts Publishing Group
Carmelite House
50 Victoria Embankment
London EC4Y 0DZ

An Hachette UK Company.
www.hachette.co.uk

www.franklinwatts.co.uk

MECHANIC MIKE'S MACHINES DIGGERS
was produced for Franklin Watts by
David West Children's Books, 6 Princeton Court, 55 Felsham Road, London SW15 1AZ

Mechanic Mike says:
Mike will tell you
something more about
the machine.

 Find out what type
of engine drives
the machine.

 Discover
something you
didn't know.

 Size dimensions
are supplied here.

 Find out how
heavy it is.

 Get your
amazing
fact here!

Contents

Bulldozer

These powerful, large earth movers are usually first on a new building site. They push away rubble and piles of earth and rocks.

Cab

Giant ripper

Giant **diesel engines** power the drive wheel at the back of the machine.

Did you know bulldozers have a giant ripper at the back? They use this to tear up tree roots, boulders, concrete and **asphalt**.

These massive machines are over 9.1 metres long.

Bulldozers can weigh up to 90 metric tons. That's the same as 15 African elephants.

Bulldozers with air-conditioned sealed cabs are used to fight wildfires. They can push trees and plants out of the way to stop the fire from spreading.

Caterpillar track

Mechanic Mike says:
Caterpillar tracks, also called crawler tracks, allow the bulldozer to move over rough, uneven ground.

5

Wheel Loader

These machines use a giant bucket to scoop up loads. They can raise the bucket up and dump the load into another truck.

Bucket

These vehicles use powerful diesel engines to drive the wheels.

Did you know the largest rubber-tyred wheel loader in the world is Le Tourneau's L-2350? Its bucket can carry more than 363 metric tons.

This medium-sized vehicle is 7.5 metres long.

It weighs 17.2 metric tons. That's about three African elephants.

Wheel loaders are also called bucket loaders, front loaders, front end loaders, pay-loaders and scoop, shovel and skip loaders.

Mechanic Mike says:
Loaders with wheels are called wheel loaders and loaders with tracks are called track loaders.

Backhoe

These tractor-like diggers do many different jobs. They have a bucket on the front and a backhoe digger at the back. Stabiliser arms at the rear keep it level when it digs.

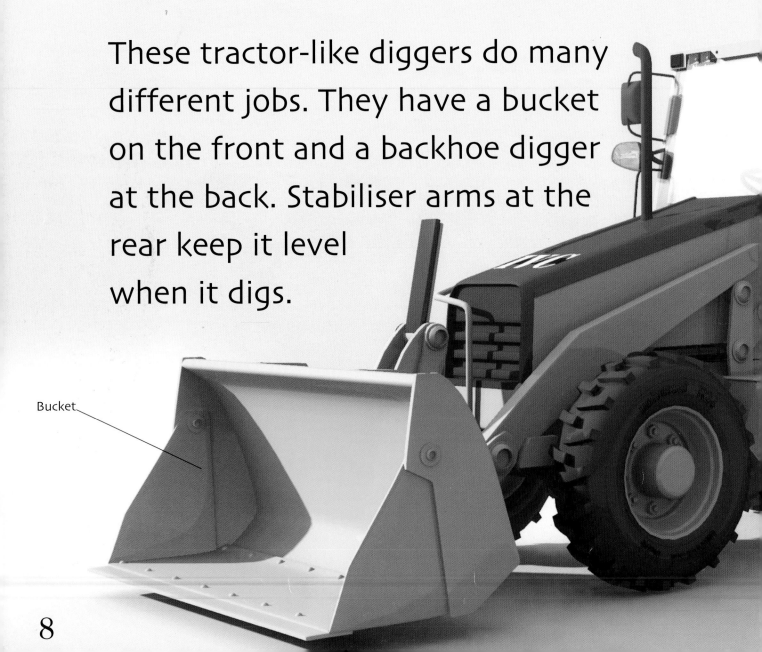

Bucket

The digger at the back can be replaced with other tools, such as a drill or **grapple**.

Did you know the machine usually has a seat that can swivel round backwards to use the backhoe controls?

This machine weighs 7.7 metric tons. That's slightly more than a large African elephant.

Backhoe loaders are usually about 6 metres long.

It has a diesel engine that powers the wheels and the **hydraulic rams**.

Backhoe digger

Stabiliser arm

Mechanic Mike says:
Backhoe is a shorter name for a backhoe loader. They are also called JCBs after the company that invented them.

9

The large diesel engine powers the drive wheels for the tracks and hydraulics.

Did you know the arm and bucket are powered by hydraulic rams? Liquid is forced into a cylinder which pushes a piston that moves the hinged arm.

Medium-sized excavators like this one are about 15.2 metres long when the arm is extended.

It weighs 31.3 metric tons. That's the same as about five African elephants.

Excavators are also called 360-degree excavators. This is because the cab and arm unit, called the 'house', can turn all the way round.

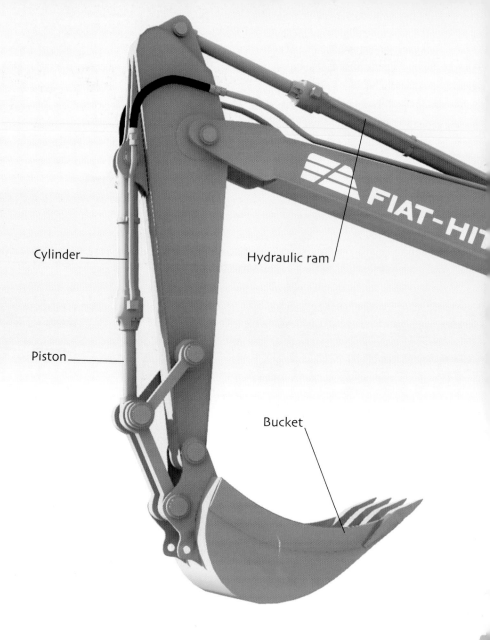

Cylinder

Hydraulic ram

Piston

Bucket

FIAT-HIT

Mechanic Mike says:
Excavators can also be used for demolition work. Their long arms are ideal for pulling down the walls of houses and offices.

Excavator

Excavators are used on **construction** sites. Their powerful arms with claw-like buckets dig trenches and **foundations** for buildings.

Scraper

These strange-looking machines are usually seen on motorway construction sites. They scrape over the earth and carry away the soil.

Mechanic Mike says:
The soil a scraper has collected might be unloaded gradually to fill hollows or released in a huge pile to make embankments.

To slice into the earth a giant scraper is pushed 30 centimetres into the ground. It acts like a giant butter knife.

They can weigh up to 48 metric tons. That's more than six African elephants.

Scrapers are long vehicles that measure up to 15.2 metres long.

These powerful machines have two diesel engines. One at the front powers the cab. The second is at the back and powers the rear wheels.

Did you know that scrapers often get stuck and need a bulldozer to push them out?

Scraper

13

Roller

Rollers, or compactors, are used to squash down earth, gravel or asphalt during the building of a road or motorway.

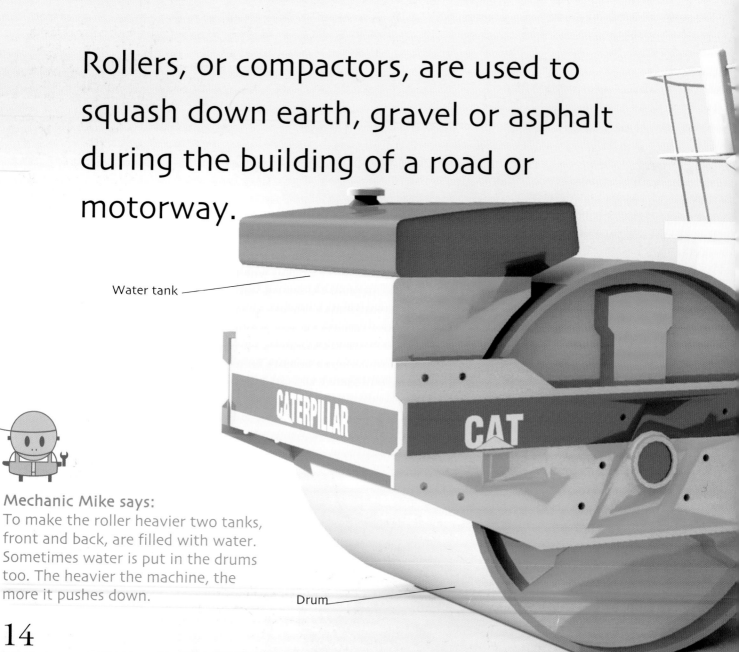

Water tank

Drum

Mechanic Mike says:
To make the roller heavier two tanks, front and back, are filled with water. Sometimes water is put in the drums too. The heavier the machine, the more it pushes down.

14

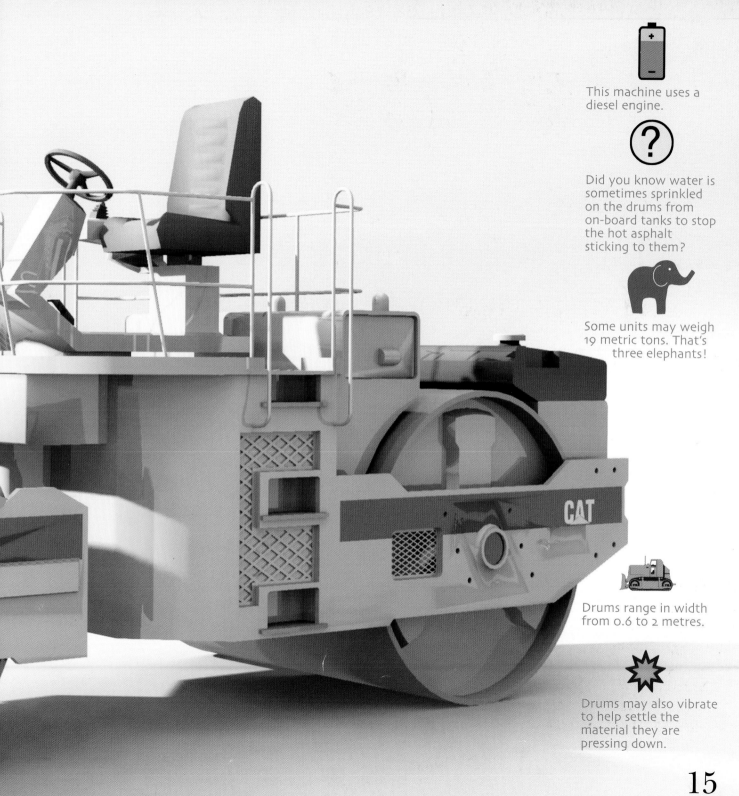

This machine uses a diesel engine.

Did you know water is sometimes sprinkled on the drums from on-board tanks to stop the hot asphalt sticking to them?

Some units may weigh 19 metric tons. That's three elephants!

Drums range in width from 0.6 to 2 metres.

Drums may also vibrate to help settle the material they are pressing down.

15

Mini Excavator

Some diggers are built in mini sizes. They can work in places that larger machines cannot fit. They are mainly used to dig trenches for pipes and cables along roadsides.

Mechanic Mike says:
A small mini excavator can fit through a house's front door.

Cab

Levers

Smaller excavators are powered by diesel engines.

Did you know two small levers on each side are used to control the excavating arm?

They weigh around 1.5 metric tons.

This machine measures less than 3 metres in length.

To protect their ears drivers wear **ear defenders** when they work in an open cab.

Skid Steer

This machine can work in small spaces. By reversing its wheels on one side and driving forwards on the other, it can spin around on the spot.

Bucket

Mechanic Mike says:
Like many machines in this book, the skid steer can change the tool on its arm to perform other tasks.

The skid steer is powered by a small diesel engine.

Did you know that skid steers don't have steering wheels? They are steered with hand levers.

This skid steer weighs 0.76 metric tons.

The skid steer measures about 3 metres long.

Skid steers can be used to dig with a bucket or to lift things with a forklift attachment. It even has a brush for sweeping up.

19

Mining Shovel

These massive diggers are used to cut away coal or oil shale from the walls of **open-cast mines**. The massive bucket has replaceable, self-sharpening teeth, which bite into the rock.

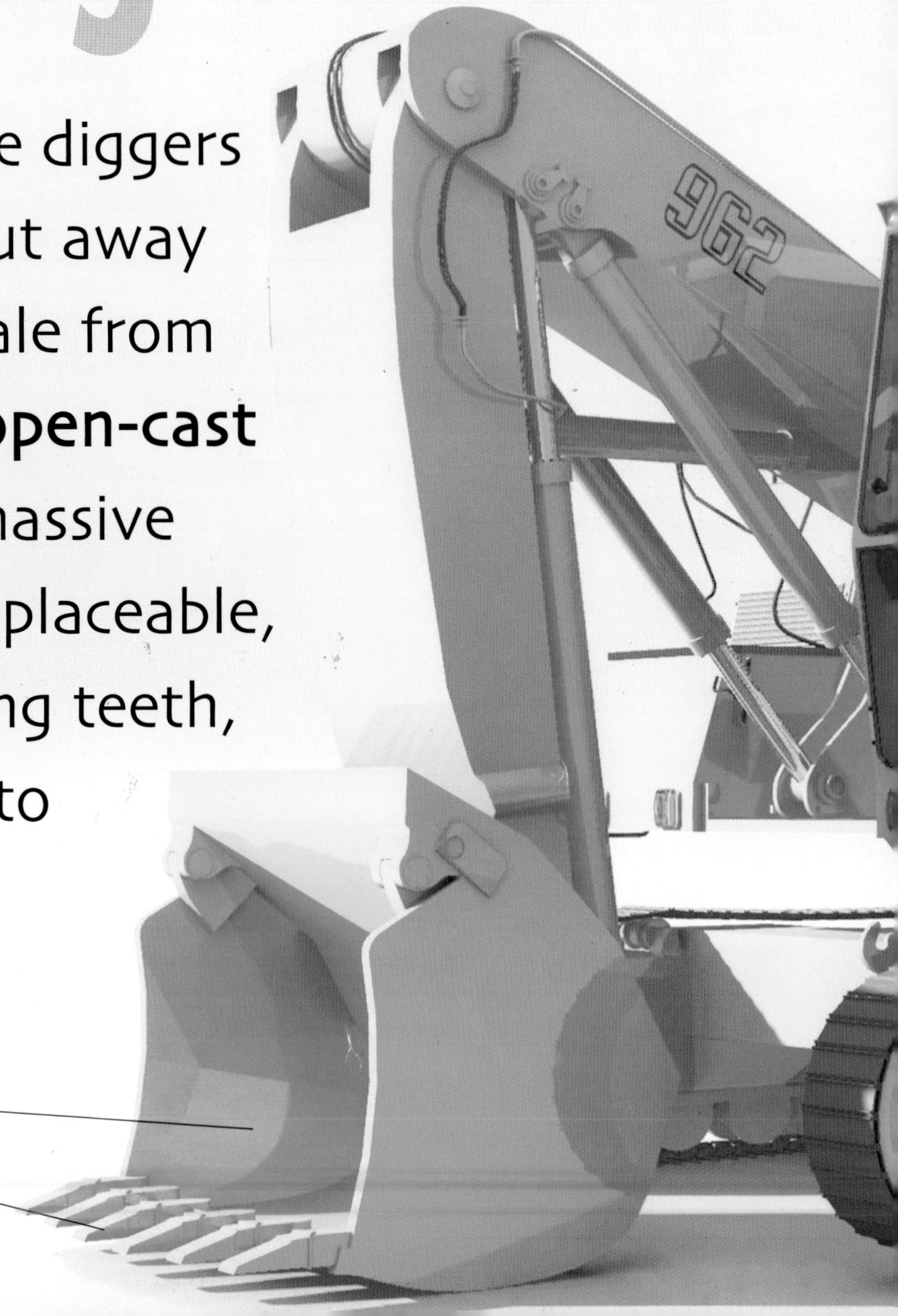

Bucket

Self-sharpening teeth

Did you know that this mining shovel can fill the back of a giant **dump truck** in under two minutes?

 This machine is 13.4 metres long.

 Mining shovels like this one can weigh up to 480 metric tons. That's about 65 large African elephants.

 Mining shovels have two large diesel engines. If one breaks down it can still run on one while the other is being repaired.

 It can run at full speed for three hours.

LIEBHERR 962

Mechanic Mike says: These machines use computers that measure and control the engine and shovel.

21

Bucket-Wheel

Bucket-wheel excavators (BWEs) are used in large-scale open-cast mines. The large wheel of buckets continuously scoops up material as the wheel turns.

These machines can move 240,000 cubic metres of earth in a day.

Did you know BWEs are the largest moving land machines ever built?

A combination of diesel and electric engines are used to power this mighty machine.

A BWE weighs in at 14,200 metric tons. That's a lot of elephants!

BWEs can be 96 metres tall and 225 metres long.

Wheel of buckets

Mechanic Mike says:
Each bucket-wheel is over 21.3 metres across.

23

Glossary

asphalt
A thick, black substance, used for making roads.

caterpillar tracks
A steel band around the wheels of a vehicle, for travel on rough ground.

construction
The process of building.

diesel engines
Engines using diesel fuel.

dump truck
A heavy truck used for transporting rock and earth.

ear defenders
Earmuffs worn to protect eardrums from noise.

foundations
The base of buildings, dug deep into the ground.

grapple
A hook or claw used to catch or hold something.

hydraulic ram
A machine's 'mechanical muscle'. Fluid enters at one end, which pushes a piston. When fluid enters at the other end it pushes the piston back. The piston moves a mechanical arm.

open-cast mine
An area of land dug into to extract coal or ore.

Index